DISCARD

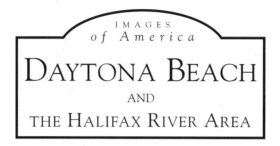

IMAGES
of America

DAYTONA BEACH
AND
THE HALIFAX RIVER AREA

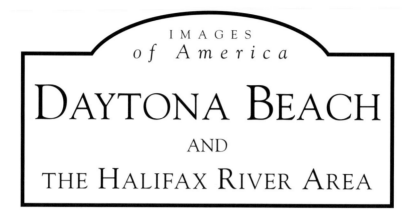

IMAGES
of America

DAYTONA BEACH
AND
THE HALIFAX RIVER AREA

Cheryl Atwell and Vincent Clarida

ARCADIA

Published by Arcadia Publishing,
an imprint of Tempus Publishing, Inc.
2 Cumberland Street
Charleston, SC 29401

Printed in Great Britain.

Library of Congress Catalog Card Number: 98-87772

For all general information contact Arcadia Publishing at:
Telephone 843-853-2070
Fax 843-853-0044
E-Mail arcadia@charleston.net

For customer service and orders:
Toll-Free 1-888-313-BOOK

Visit us on the internet at http://www.arcadiaimages.com

CONTENTS

4/09

This aerial view of the Daytona Beach area shows the downtown, City Island, bridges, and the peninsula in the 1960s.

INTRODUCTION

Daytona Beach and the Halifax River area have a rich and colorful history. Explorers from Spain, colonists from France, and settlers from England have all left their imprint on the region as sovereignty shifted from one European government to another.

The first plantation to be built in this area was the Mount Oswald plantation, located in present-day Ormond Beach. Later, the Spanish offered land grants to those willing to plant and cultivate the lands, which resulted in the Bulow, Dunlawton, and Williams plantations being established along the Halifax River. The planters found the area ideal for growing sugar cane, indigo, rice, and cotton. The plantations flourished until the Seminole Indian Wars. In 1835, the Native Americans burned all the plantations, and the terrified owners fled back to the north.

The Halifax area became mostly abandoned until after the Civil War, except for the live oak trade. This area was abundant with majestic live oak trees, of which selected limbs were ideal for specific parts of a ship's frame. Each winter, hearty work crews, who became known as "Live Oakers," would sail from New England to Mosquito Inlet (now Ponce Inlet) and set up camps along the Halifax River. There, the crews would harvest the live oak trees used for shipbuilding in the north.

After the devastation caused by the Civil War, pioneers came to Florida to start a new life. The Halifax area was ideal because of its rivers, beach, and nearby access to the ocean, via the inlet. Orange groves were soon established. Goods were brought in by schooner and unloaded at the inlet. The few roads were only sandy trails, making the Halifax River the main transportation route. Nearly every family had a small sailboat at that time.

In 1870, Matthias Day came from Mansfield, Ohio, and purchased the Samuel Williams grant, which contained 3,200 acres. He laid out a small town along the Halifax River, which was later named Daytona in his honor when it became incorporated in July 1876.

The earliest problems that faced the newly elected officials of this new community included drainage, drinking water, and mosquitoes. Drainage canals were constructed in order to drain the low-lying areas. There were epidemics of malaria and yellow fever when surface and storage tanks were in vogue, but with the discovery of artesian wells, this menace disappeared.

Bridges were built across the river, opening up the peninsula for development, and the railroad came to Daytona in 1886. This opened up the lines of trade and communication with cities to the north, and a new industry began to emerge. Men with vision started to build large hotels to accommodate affluent tourists, anxious to visit the area. These resorts catered to their guests' every need. The Daytona area became known as a prime resort community, offering swimming, boating, fishing, hunting, polo, lawn bowling, archery, shuffleboard, and more.

Among the most notable hotels were the Ormond, the Clarendon, the Princess Issena, the Coquina, and the Riviera. One of the most popular attractions promoted by the hotels were jungle cruises down the Tomoka River. Passenger boats with names such as *Tomoka* and *Uncle Sam* would meander down the pristine river, revealing exotic wildlife, including alligators, turtles, and birds, which thrived there. Tourists couldn't wait to tell their friends up north about their adventures.

In 1896, Charles Grover Burgoyne, a wealthy New York printer, arrived in Daytona and became the city's outstanding benefactor. He provided band concerts for the public, built a lighted concrete sidewalk along the river, built a community center, and was active in all aspects of community life. He was elected commodore of the Halifax River Yacht Club and mayor of Daytona. Much of Daytona's early tourist trade can be attributed to Burgoyne's vision.

Shortly after the turn of the century, motor cars became available. At first, the cars were toys for rich men who wanted to see just how fast they could go. These enthusiasts soon discovered that the beach, with its hard-packed sand, made an ideal racecourse.

The measured mile was established, and each year starting in 1903, men from the U.S. and Europe would bring their cars to race on the sand. Special cars were built for attempts to establish new land speed records on the sands of Ormond and Daytona. The publicity became widespread, and the area became known as the "Birthplace of Speed" and the "World's Most Famous Beach." The beach was also shared with early aviation pioneers, who used the beach as the area's first airport. During the early 1900s, passenger rides were offered to those visitors who wanted to experience the thrill of flying. Automobile and motorcycle races were held on the beach for many years. In 1936, a beach/road course was established, superceded in 1948 by a larger course, near Ponce de Leon Inlet. This course was abandoned in 1959 with the opening of the Daytona International Speedway.

Consolidated Daytona Beach came into existence in 1926 when Daytona, Daytona Beach, and Seabreeze merged under a single government. The area was very active during the 1920s, and the great Florida land boom resulted in the building of grand subdivisions such as the Daytona Highlands, Rio Vista, and Gannymeade. Real estate activity became rampant, and speculators came in droves. This all came to an end with the destructive hurricanes of 1926 and 1928, and the Great Depression in 1929.

The 1930s government WPA (Works Project Administration) projects included the construction of the boardwalk and bandshell, and helped to reduce unemployment in the area. The United States entry into World War II provided an economic boost in the 1940s through military contracts given to the Daytona Boat Works to build boats for the Navy. Daytona was also selected as the site for the second WAC Training Center, where 16,000 WAC's were trained from 1942 to 1944. Most of the large hotels were taken over by the military to house the women until a training center could be built. The city airport was converted into a naval air station, for the training of Navy pilots, until 1945.

The passage of time travels at an alarming rate and we risk losing all touch with our past. It is our hope that by sharing the photographs included in this book, we will create an interest in our area's colorful past, and encourage preservation of historic photographs, documents, and memorabilia.

The photographs included here are only a few of the many wonderful old scenes preserved by photographers who preceded us in Daytona and the Halifax River area. Among these men are Richard LeSesne, William Coursen, Edward G. Harris, Lawson Diggett, and others, who have provided us with a priceless heritage. The images selected for this book came from the collection housed at the Halifax Historical Museum, a non-profit organization whose mission is to collect, preserve, display, and interpret artifacts that tell the history of Daytona Beach and the Halifax River area.

One

PIONEERS, PEOPLE, AND PLACES

William Jackson and Charles Dougherty are shown in front of Jackson's store in 1880. Jackson was one of the area's first merchants and was an influential politician, being elected to the first Common Council of Daytona in 1876. His store was the site of the signing of the incorporation of Daytona on July 26, 1876.

Matthias Day was the owner of the tract of land, consisting of 2,142 acres, which was later named Daytona in his honor. Day came here from Ohio with a dream of building a city in the beautiful forest land along the Halifax River. He laid out streets and large lots for homes along Ridgewood Avenue, which at that time was a narrow dirt lane atop a ridge line of magnificent moss-draped oak trees.

After purchasing the land, Day returned to Ohio to gather men and machinery to start a colony. On his return he set up a sawmill and built the first hotel in Daytona, which he called the Colony House. He was unable to meet the payments on the land and eventually returned to the North. Day is shown standing to the right with his family at the beautiful Fairchild Oak, one of the largest trees still standing in Florida.

Standing to the left are D.D. Rogers and his son, C.M. Rogers, and his survey crew. D.D. Rogers was one of the first land surveyors in Florida. He laid out the boundaries of Daytona and many other cities in Florida. A man of vision, he also built a home, planted orange groves, sold real estate, built the area's first ice plant, and originated the idea of building bridges across the Halifax River. His ancestors still live in Daytona Beach today.

One of the pioneers in Daytona was C.M. Wilder, who built one of the first great homes on South Beach Street at Live Oak Avenue. He and his family are seen here in the front yard of their home. Famous author and screenwriter Robert Wilder was C.M. Wilder's nephew.

Shown here is the inside of the Wilder home, in a photograph taken at the turn of the century by Richard LeSesne, a local professional photographer. The lighting in the photograph shows the interior of the beautiful home at its best. This home still stands today as a testament to the home building trade of yesteryear.

John C. Maley was the area's first blacksmith, setting up his smithy on Cedar Street, where the Maley home still stands. He was elected to the first town council in 1876, and continued to be a prominent citizen throughout his lifetime. Maley Street is named for him.

Elizabeth and John Maley had eight children—Jerome, John Jr., Fred, Robert, Esther, Belle, Madeline, and Helen. Mrs. Maley, who was the first postmaster of Daytona, is shown here with all her granddaughters in this unusual 1902 family portrait.

13

In 1875, Mrs. Mary Hoag came to the area with her family from Cincinnati and purchased the Colony House, renaming it the Palmetto House because of its thatched palmetto roof. Mrs. Hoag was the sister of Lorenzo Huston and a member of the Pope/Davidson family.

Lorenzo D. Huston was a Methodist minister who had long flowing hair and a beard trimmed in the Robert E. Lee style. He came here with the father and uncles of C.M. Wilder in 1875. Huston had the distinction of being elected as the first mayor of Daytona in 1876. His son Menefee, a Confederate veteran, was also elected to the first town council and was the town's first druggist.

Laurence Thompson came to this area in 1875 and established the second general store in Daytona, also located on Beach Street. He helped to found the Congregational Church, started the area's first building and loan company (where he served as manager), and opened the first real estate and insurance business.

This photograph shows the Thompson store and house as they looked in 1875. At that time Beach Street was a narrow, dirt road paved with crushed oyster shell. Additions were added to the store and it was converted into a home. It was once owned by famous author, playwright, and editor Harrison Garfield Rhodes. The home stands today as the oldest home in Daytona and is presently owned by Dr. William Doremus.

Lilian Thompson, daughter of Laurence Thompson, is shown on the left with her mother and her friend, Clare Wilkinson, in front of her home. Lilian was a teacher and never married.

Lilian's Place was the first home built on the peninsula, located at what is now the north side of Orange Avenue, on the Halifax River. This beautiful Victorian home was built for Lilian by her father, and it stands today as a newly renovated bed and breakfast. The home is haunted by the "honest-to-goodness" friendly ghost of a young woman named Lucile, who lived there before the turn of the century.

Dr. Josie Rogers was the daughter of D.D. Rogers. She was one of only a few women who went to college at the turn of the century, graduating in 1907. She went on to become the first woman doctor in Daytona, practicing until 1947. She was interested in her community, became active in politics, and was elected mayor in 1922. She died in 1975 at the age of 98, and to this day she is the only woman mayor of Daytona Beach.

J.E. Rawlings is seen here in his World War I uniform. His was among those first families to settle in Daytona. He graduated from college and became a doctor, starting his practice here in January of 1905.

In 1904 the Rawlings family purchased this Colonial Revival masonry home on South Beach Street. In 1948 the property was donated to the county and it served as the Courthouse Annex until 1973. The building now serves as the County Beach Management Office headquarters.

18

Mary McLeod Bethune, the daughter of a freed slave, had a vision as a young woman to start a school for black girls. She started the Daytona Normal School for Girls in 1904. This young teacher went on to become a good friend and advisor to Eleanor Roosevelt during President Franklin Roosevelt's administration. The school is now the co-educational Bethune-Cookman College in Daytona Beach.

This is Cookman Hall at Bethune Cookman College as it appeared in days gone by. It was one of the original buildings on the campus.

In 1896 Charles Grover Burgoyne, a wealthy New York printer, arrived in Daytona and soon became the city's most outstanding benefactor. He provided band concerts in the park, donated the Burgoyne Casino and the Esplanade Burgoyne, was a sponsor of the Elks Lodge, was president of the East Coast Auto Association, commodore of the Halifax River Yacht Club, and mayor of Daytona. Much of Daytona's early tourist trade can be attributed to this man.

Charles Burgoyne's house was the largest residence in Daytona when it was built. It was located on North Beach Street fronting the river, and locals referred to it as "the castle." Those who were children at that time fondly remember walking along the stone wall surrounding the home. Unfortunately, it was demolished in 1941 to make way for a shopping center.

In 1870, John H.L. Botefuhr came to Daytona Beach from New York in a schooner laden with household goods, chickens, cats, dogs, a horse and carriage, and materials to build a house. His belongings were brought by wagon from the inlet to the land he purchased on the peninsula. A street was named for him on the South peninsula in later years.

John Andrew Bostrom was the son of Andrew Bostrom, who was the founding father of Ormond Beach. Andrew Bostrom started building his home, which he called "Bosarve," in 1868. This 10,000-square-foot house served as a haven for travelers as well as a hotel for newcomers while they built their homes. His descendants still live in Ormond, but the large home was demolished in 1946.

Henry Flagler purchased the Ormond Hotel from John Anderson and Joseph Price in 1890, at which time he increased the capacity of the hotel to 150 rooms. Flagler also purchased the White Railroad and developed it into the Florida East Coast Railroad, which brought tourism to the area.

This photo of John Anderson was taken at the Ormond Hotel. He was the one of the original owners of the hotel, along with Joseph Price. They built the hotel in 1887 on the peninsula at what is now Granada Avenue. When Anderson sold the 75-room hotel to Flagler, he and Price became the managers until their deaths in 1911.

The Ormond Hotel was a grand resort at the turn of the century, with railroad service directly to the front door. It offered one of the only swimming pools in the area, and was enjoyed by tourists from all over the world.

The Ormond Hotel was a favorite of tourists for almost 100 years. This photo was taken in 1903 and shows the main mode of transportation of that day. Partly due to its immense size, the wooden hotel fell into disrepair in later years, and was demolished in 1992, much to the dismay of locals. Much effort was spent in trying to save this famous landmark.

John D. Rockefeller was a longtime winter resident in Ormond Beach. At first he stayed at the Ormond Hotel, but soon found that he was being charged more because of his great wealth. He purchased the home across the street from the hotel, and named it "The Casements." Mr. Rockefeller was famous locally for passing out dimes to children on the streets. Some present-day residents who were children then still remember him fondly.

The Casements was the winter home of John D. Rockefeller for many years, and was reported to be his favorite home. He named the house The Casements because of the many casement windows in the home. The beautiful home has been restored in recent years and serves as a cultural arts community center for Ormond Beach.

The famous local rumrunner Bill McCoy owned the schooner *Arethusa* which, along with other schooners, was used to smuggle rum from the Bahamas during Prohibition. In 1923 he was caught and his ship impounded in New York. He served a short jail sentence, but when he was released, went back to smuggling. McCoy dealt only with the best bootleg liquor, and any merchandise bought from him was said to be "The Real McCoy," thus coining the now famous phrase.

The *Arethusa* was one of several schooners captained by the famous rumrunner Bill McCoy. It is shown here anchored in the Halifax River in the 1920s.

Brownie was the town's mascot. He arrived in about 1940 and was adopted by the townsfolk. He had a very good disposition, and was loved by everyone. He had his own bank account to pay for his food and vet bills, and even his own tombstone when he died in 1954. He is buried in Riverfront Park, with a fitting memorial.

Two

HISTORIC POTPOURRI

The ruins of the Dunlawton Sugar Mill Plantation are seen here in this photograph taken in the 1950s. This was one of the plantations along the coast of Florida built in the early 1800s for the production of sugar. These large plantations also grew indigo, rice, and cotton, but sugar cane was the major crop grown. Today this is the site of the Sugar Mill Botanical Gardens.

These large in-ground vats at the Dunlawton Plantation were used in the processing of sugar from cane. The stalks were pressed by the use of a sugar mill to obtain juice. The juice was poured into the heated vats in a process that was used to obtain syrup and molasses.

This young man is shown standing in front of the first city hall building on South Beach Street, at Orange Avenue. This building had first been used as Daytona's first railroad station.

A young Wilkinson child sits on the rusted remains of a small sugar mill works from the Smith Plantation, located at the corner of Ridgewood and Loomis Avenue. In the 1950s the mill works were moved to the Dunlawton Sugar Mill Botanical Gardens in Port Orange.

This 1900 photo shows Beach Street from the South Bridge (now Orange Avenue). The small building on the left of the bridge was the jail at that time. The building on the right was used as the first railroad station, city hall, library, telephone office, and fire station. The building on the far left was the Thompson Building, which housed the Opera House.

The Halifax River Yacht Club was built in 1896. It is the oldest yacht club on the east coast of the United States still in its original location. This is how it appeared in 1931.

The Daytona Beach Main Fire Station is located next door to the Yacht Club at the corner of Orange Avenue and Beach Street. It was built in 1925 and looks much the same today as it did when it was first built. This 1929 photograph was taken by Richard LeSesne. The building, with its beautiful Spanish architecture, remains a city landmark.

The Burgoyne Casino was built in 1915, not as a gambling casino, but as a community center, and was presented as a gift to the town by benefactor Charles G. Burgoyne. It served as the home of the chamber of commerce as well as a recreational center. Dances, shuffleboard, cards, checkers, and horseshoes were offered as entertainment to the tourists and local residents. It burned to the ground under mysterious circumstances in 1937.

The Kress Building, located on North Beach Street, was built in 1932 and was constructed in the Neo-Gothic architectural style. It was originally built as a 5 and 10 cent store, and today houses retail stores and office space.

The United States Post Office building was built in 1933 on North Beach Street. Its Spanish-style architecture blended with other downtown structures. The building has been restored and has been placed on the National Register of Historic Places.

This 1926 photo shows the impressive entrance arch for the large resort subdivision called Gannymede, which was planned for South Daytona during the 1920s land boom. The arch, built in 1924, was demolished in 1961 to make way for the widening of Ridgewood Avenue. The subdivision never reached the heights which its developer envisioned.

During the Florida land boom, the Tarragona Arch was built at the entrance to the exclusive Daytona Coquina Highlands subdivision, at what is now White Street and International Speedway Blvd. The center tower housed the real estate offices and included a fireplace and powder room. One of the gateways was removed in 1942 to make way for road widening. The remaining portion of the arch was recently moved back 75 feet to accommodate further widening of the road. The city is currently in the process of having it restored to its original beauty.

St. Mary's Episcopal Church is located at the corner of Orange Avenue and Ridgewood Avenue. It was built in 1883, and was the first mission in Daytona. It received its name because of an engraver's error, changing the name from St. Marks to St. Mary's. This photograph shows how the Victorian building looked at the turn of the century.

St. Paul's Catholic Church is a huge and magnificent structure located on Ridgewood Avenue and was built in 1927. Its Mediterranean-style architecture stands out against the Daytona skyline in a unique reflection of yesteryear in this 1937 photograph. It is the oldest Catholic church in the area.

The *Nathan Cobb* was a three-masted schooner that ran aground at Ormond Beach during a storm in 1896. The cargo was washed overboard and salvaged by the locals. The ship disintegrated in the surf, and the wood from the hull was salvaged. The outline of the remaining pieces of the hull can be seen in the sand today when the surf has washed the beach clean after a storm.

The Nathan Cobb Cottage was built on Orchard Lane behind the Ormond Hotel from wood salvaged from the wreck of the *Nathan Cobb*. It has been recently restored by a local former lifeguard who makes it his home today.

Commodore Charles Grover Burgoyne was the most important benefactor of Daytona in his day. He was born in 1847 and died in 1916. He is buried at the Pinewood Cemetery, which is located on Main Street and Peninsula Avenue. The Italian marble angel headstone was placed on his grave by his wife, Mary Therese. Vandals destroyed the angel in 1941, and it has never been replaced.

The beautiful Pinewood Cemetery is one of the oldest cemeteries in the Daytona area, and certainly the oldest on the peninsula. The coquina and wrought-iron gates mark the entrance to the burial places of some of Daytona's most prominent pioneer citizens of yesteryear.

36

The majesty Ponce de Leon Lighthouse was built of red brick, and its beacon was first lit November 1, 1887. It was originally called the Light Station at Mosquito Inlet. It has 203 steps that spiral the interior, which reaches to 175 feet in height. It was one of the first lighthouses in Florida. The original beacon lamp burned oil, but the lamp was converted to electricity in the 1933. Today the lighthouse is the centerpiece of the Ponce de Leon Lighthouse Museum complex.

The Florida East Coast Automobile Club was built at Silver Beach on the peninsula and formerly opened on July 4, 1904. It was intended to be a focal point for the annual auto meet, and to be a physical starting point for the races. Its members were influential in bringing famous people and tourists from many countries to this area to compete in and see the speed trials.

This unique three-headed palm tree was located at Ridgewood Avenue and Volusia Avenue. Due to widening of the road, it was transplanted in the 1940s next to city hall, and unfortunately did not survive the transplanting.

The famous Big Tree was located on what is now Big Tree Road in South Daytona, near the entrance to the current Palm Grove subdivision. This huge oak tree was 36 feet in circumference, 100 feet in height, and its branches spread out 157 feet from its center. A platform was built in it so that the many tourists visiting every year could enjoy its beauty and the view from it.It eventually succumbed due to fire and disease.

Three
MAKING A LIVING

This ox cart, shown here on Beach Street in an early Harris photo, was used to haul cut timber to the train station, seen in the background on the left.

William Jackson owned the first general store in Daytona. The store, built around 1870 by W.P. Burr, was located on South Beach Street and sold goods of all kinds. Jackson received the goods at his dock on the river as they were brought down from Jacksonville. The locals depended on his store for just about all their needs.

The Peck and Foster general store was located at the corner of Beach Street and Loomis Avenue. The Peck home can be seen on the left, and the Garland home is on the right. Burt Foster is standing to the right, J.H.L. Botefuhr is in the center, and Will Rich is sitting on the left.

This photo shows the interior of a gift shop located on Beach Street in the 1930s. Gift shops began to appear in this area with the influx of tourists that came to the area in the winters for the beach racing.

The Moore Brothers Dry Goods Store was in existence from 1897 to 1907. The store was located on the corner of Beach and Bay Streets and shared the building with a drug store, which later became Hankins Drug Store. Pictured here are William and Marice Moore (the owners), William's son Carlyle (with his dog), Emma Moore, Gail Moore, Marve Moore, and Henry Schmidt (in bicycle togs).

Early citrus groves were planted among mature hardwood oaks and palms. Here family members are picking oranges in the late 1800s.

The citrus industry became a huge industry in Florida starting in the late 1800s and still exists as one of the major industries today. Oranges, tangerines, and grapefruit are grown in south and central Florida. Harvest time is in the fall, and citrus is plentiful all winter long. Great freezes have hurt the industry several times, but so far it has always been able to come back to produce the best and sweetest citrus in the country.

Gene Johnson, on the right, was an enterprising fellow who ran a sporting goods shop, rented bicycles, and made bicycle repairs on Beach Street from approximately 1915 until the 1940s.

Lots at the turn of the century were a bargain by today's standards, as seen in this photograph of James Wilkinson. A lot of comparable size today would cost between $25,000 and $50,000!

During the Florida land boom in the 1920s, speculators sold property to anyone with money. Sometimes the land was above water, sometimes it wasn't. The sign proclaims that all kinds of fruits and vegetables can be grown on this land. These tracts were sold in 5, 10, or 20-acre parcels, and attracted many unsuspecting northerners.

Richard LeSesne was considered the premier local professional photographer in the 1920s, 1930s, and 1940s. He took many of the beautiful photographs contained in this book, focusing on local happenings in the area. He came to Daytona in 1903 from Clarksville, Georgia. He died in 1946 in Daytona Beach, but his legacy lives on in his beautiful photographs.

This is LeSesne's Photography Studio on Palmetto Avenue as it appeared in the 1920s.

This Austin sales and service center was located on Ridgewood Avenue in Daytona. The Austin was a popular car here in the 1920s and 1930s.

The Swanson Brothers Auto Painting shop was located on South Street, and was considered the place to have your car painted. Shown here in this 1930s photograph are Roosevelt and Sebring Swanson, and J.C. McMillan.

Agriculture was and is a thriving business here. Three seasons of growing produce crops of vegetables such as corn, potatoes, tomatoes, celery, cabbage, carrots, and more. Another major crop here besides citrus is the fern industry. A large part of the country's florist ferns are grown on farms in Volusia and surrounding counties. Potatoes are being dug on the McDonald Farm in this photograph taken in the 1930s.

This "Florida Bicycle," which was really a type of cart with two large wheels, was pulled by a mule or ox, and hauled timber for the "Live Oakers" who came to Florida every winter to cut trees for the shipbuilders in New England.

47

This beautiful beaux arts building was the first bank built in Daytona in 1910. It began as the Merchant's Bank and operated until the Great Depression. It became the Florida Bank and Trust in 1936 and was called that until the 1960s. In 1951 local artists Don Emery and his son Don painted five huge murals on the inside north wall depicting scenes of the area. When the Florida National Bank moved to its new and larger office on Ridgewood Avenue, this building was deserted. It remained empty many years, with a few attempts to make it a gift shop and a restaurant, until it was purchased by the Halifax Historical Society in 1984. It opened its doors in 1986 as the Halifax Historical Museum and remains in their care to this day. The interior boasts original architecture of stained-glass windows and skylights, decorative carved plaster, beautiful mahogany, brass, and lighting. It is on the National Register of Historic Places.

Four

PLAYTIMES AND PASTIMES

This is one of the champion whippets that ran in the dog races on the beach sponsored by the Riviera Hotel in the 1920s. The races were the early version of the greyhound races now held at the Daytona Beach Kennel Club on U.S. 92 in Daytona. This great image was taken by local photographer Richard LeSesne.

Guests at the Riviera Hotel had many diversions to keep them occupied during their stay. Archery was one of the many pastimes offered. Other offerings were shuffleboard, lawn bowling, croquet, horseback riding, boating, fishing, and skeet shooting.

Young women are shown here dancing on the beach at the water's edge in the 1920s. This is another of Richard LeSesne's wonderful photographic offerings.

The Wilder family entertains with a lawn party in the late 1800s. The ladies shown here are dressed in their finery and dancing the minuet to music provided by local musicians.

In this nostalgic photograph, Daytona schoolchildren are seen dancing around the Maypole for the annual May Day festivities at their school in the 1890s.

Children often enacted adult parts in Tom Thumb weddings, which were held as fund-raisers for various organizations. This "wedding" took place in Daytona in 1925.

Members of the Burgoyne Games Club are enjoying a game of "Barnyard Golf" in this image taken on the grounds of the Burgoyne Casino in 1930. Playing horseshoes was a favorite pastime of the gentlemen at that time.

Ormond Hotel Golf Club members are enjoying a round of golf in the early 1920s with famous visitor Will Rogers, holding the club at the center of the photograph. Many famous guests stayed at the resorts in the Daytona area in the 1920s and 1930s.

Beauty pageants were popular in Daytona from the 1920s until the 1970s. The Miss Florida Pageants were sometimes held here, and Miss Florida and the runner-up are shown in this photo taken in 1936. In the 1940s, 1950s, and 1960s, the Miss Dixie Pageant was held at the Bandshell on the boardwalk.

This beauty contest of the mid-1920s was held on the beach to promote some of the new subdivisions of the Florida land boom period. Represented here are Miss El Pino Parque, Miss Inlet Terrace, Miss Wilbur By the Sea, Miss Kalinway Heights, Miss Daytona Highlands, Miss Seabreeze, and Miss Ortona. The building behind them is the Pier Casino at Main Street.

A giant jewfish is shown here in a 1931 photograph. The fish weighed 650 pounds and was 6 feet 10 inches long. The angler is Allen Hargrove. Fishing served as a significant recreational pastime as well as a business to supply food for the locals.

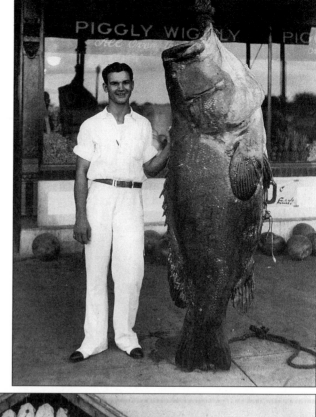

This catch of red bass has a total weight of 1,450 pounds, and was caught by 31 fisherman off the Keating Pier on August 7, 1902, during a three-hour period. The fish were as large as the little girl seen at the bottom right of the photograph.

Mr. and Mrs. Smith are showing off their 15-pound and 22-pound red snappers caught aboard the *Mary Beth* fishing boat on March 22, 1938. The photograph was taken on the City Docks in the Halifax River downtown.

A giant manta ray is displayed at the Halifax River Yacht Club by the fisherman who caught it on a fishing expedition out of the Ponce de Leon Inlet in the 1930s.

A trio of fisherman display their catch of silver tarpon at the Burgoyne Casino in this 1920s image. Sporting goods shop owner Gene Johnson is standing in the back of the truck.

These young men had a good day's catch while surf fishing at Ponce de Leon Inlet in the 1930s. It was not unusual to catch 100 fish in one outing. There are approximately 125 fish in this photograph.

The Daytona Band was the area's first band. The volunteer musicians put on public concerts and played for street dances on Main and Beach Streets. They later played at the Burgoyne Casino. This photo was taken in 1902 in front of the Thomas Goodall home.

The Saracina Virtuoso Concert Band from New York was hired by Commodore Charles Burgoyne to give two daily concerts for the benefit of the tourists and locals during the winter seasons. The band first performed at the riverfront gazebo at Orange and Beach Streets, then at the Burgoyne Casino after it was built.

This wedding party was photographed in front of St. Mary's Church on May 21, 1926. The bride was Frances Davidson Brower, and the groom, who is not in the photo, was Lionel J. Martoccia. The bridesmaids were Juanita Messmore, Catherine Johnson, and Mary Gille.

The Daytona High School basketball team is shown here in front of the Daytona High School (later Mainland High School) in 1915. From left to right are the following: (seated) Raymond Green, Curtis Gardiner, and Quinn Brauch; (standing) John Wetherell, Wienthrop Esch, George Marks, and John Milligan.

This Seabreeze High School baseball team was photographed here in 1924. The players are Walter McBride, Millard Campbell, Frank Tyner, Coach Ossinsky, Henry Wilcox, Keith Earl, Bunny Stuart, Mortimer Courtney, Floyd Stuart, Lawrence Johnson, Roy Embry, Ed Seeley, Cecil Grant, and Ethan Viall.

Shuffleboard tournaments on City Island were popular pastimes in the early 1930s, and the courts are still being used today. The Burgoyne Casino can be seen in the background in this photograph.

Boxing matches were held on the beach near the boardwalk in the early 1930s. Many different events were held on the beach here at one time or another.

Lawn bowling matches were held at the Daytona Lawn Bowling Club on City Island. Lawn bowling was a very popular sport here during the 1920s and 1930s. Some of the tourists would come to the area just to participate in the tournaments.

The Daytona Model Midget Raceway was built on City Island in 1948 for local model race car enthusiasts. The miniature cars were tethered by a small steel cable and ran individually around a 70-foot circular track. The cars were powered by large model airplane engines, which were connected to the wheels through a set of gears. The speeds reached up to 140 mph. The raceway was a popular attraction for locals and tourists alike.

Five
HOSPITALITY FLORIDA STYLE

This 1911 photograph shows the Geneva Hotel, which was located on Ocean Boulevard near the beach. Mr. William Clark is behind the wheel, and seated next to him is Mrs. Frank Stingle, who was the owner of the hotel.

Daytona founder Matthias Day built this hotel on South Beach Street and called it the Colony House. It was used to house newcomers to the town until they could build their own home. When the schooner from Jacksonville failed to bring the shingles in time for the opening, the roof was covered with thatched palmetto fronds. The name was later changed to the Palmetto House because of this roof. The structure burned down in August of 1922.

Dr. James Rose built the Ridgewood Hotel in 1894 as a fashionable resort for those attending the early beach races. Sir Malcolm Campbell and Major H.O.D. Segrave were two of the notable guests who stayed at this regal hotel. Originally a frame structure, a coquina rock front was added in 1912, which helped it to survive two major fires. It lost much of its charm when the beautiful oak trees in the front were cut down for the widening of U.S. Route 1; business failed and it was demolished in 1975.

Captain J.O. Jorstad's bi-plane is seen here on the beach in front of the Clarendon Hotel during the winter of 1919–20. Passenger rides were offered to tourists who wanted to experience the thrill of flying.

The Clarendon Hotel is shown in this 1904 image on its opening day. This large wooden structure fronted the beach at the end of Seabreeze Blvd. It was unfortunately destroyed by a spectacular fire in 1909, was replaced by a seven-story building of masonry construction, and reopened in 1911. A unique feature of this hotel was auto access to the beach via a tunnel through the base of the hotel. The hotel was referred to as the "Grand Old Lady" of the beach.

John Anderson and Joseph Price built the Ormond Hotel in 1887. Henry Flagler then bought the hotel in 1900 and greatly expanded it. He also constructed a railroad bridge across the Halifax River to bring his affluent guests to the hotel. At one time it was said to be the largest wooden structure in the United States. This photograph was taken in 1903. The hotel was later turned into a residence for senior citizens, and was eventually demolished in 1992 to make way for a luxury high-rise condominium.

The elegant Princess Issena Hotel was a regal landmark in the heart of the Daytona Beach resort area on Seabreeze Boulevard, and is shown here as it looked in 1931. The hotel was built by Mr. and Mrs. C.C. Post, who opened it in 1908. The hotel property also included an inn and separate cottages that encompassed an entire city block. It was later made into a residential resort for senior citizens, but was eventually demolished in 1981.

The Bretton Inn, which fronted the ocean at what is now Granada Boulevard in Ormond Beach, was built in 1899 by James P. Vining. Vining demolished it in 1923, and replaced it with the larger and more substantial Coquina Hotel.

The Coquina Hotel opened in 1923 and boasted many notable guests, who were treated to the finest food and service available at the time. The pink stucco building with its Moorish design was a first-class resort. Its interior included high ceilings, a pillared dining room, immense fire places, and a sunken living area in the lobby that had a balconied rotunda. The hotel was demolished in 1968 so that A1A could be widened.

The Riviera Resort Hotel was built in 1924 as part of the Rio Vista home subdivision. Its spacious grounds extended from west of U.S. 1 to the Halifax River. This once-glorious hotel catered to affluent guests who were provided with activities such as boating, tennis, golf, horseback riding, polo, skeet shooting, and more. Eventually it fell into disrepair, and in 1997 it was purchased by a group that is renovating it for an assisted living facility for seniors.

Six

LET'S GO TO THE BEACH

This man entertains a crowd at the water's edge during the 1930s by riding on one of the huge loggerhead turtles that inhabit our beaches. These turtles are on the endangered species list today, and this kind of activity will cost you a fine or land you in jail. Today the turtle's habitats are protected from people and automobiles along the entire length of the beach in Volusia County.

The Keating Pier was the first pier constructed on the beach in our area. It was built by the Keating family in the late 1800s, at the present-day site of the Main Street Pier. The original pier was constructed of palm logs and wooden planking, and boasted a gazebo at the end. It was washed away several times in storms, and was finally replaced with the more substantial pier that exists there today.

This 1890s photograph shows the bicycles and dress of the day. The hard-packed sands lured families to the beach for recreation and exercise all year long. These hardy souls reached the beach by way of boat or ferry across the river. Before the roads were built, bicyclists had to walk their bicycles across the high sand dunes stretching across the peninsula.

This group of family and friends pose for the camera in their newest swim attire in the late 1800s. Note that the women had to wear stockings, because it was not proper to show their legs in public.

Swimming attire changed somewhat through the years, as shown in this 1920 image of a group at the beach. By this time, the ladies were allowed to have bare legs if they chose, and their skirts had shortened, but the wool suits were still baggy and heavy.

The young lady in this photograph offers a treat for the horse. The horse and buggy was a practical mode of transportation on the beach in the late 1800s, before motorcars arrived.

Another popular mode of transportation was the bicycle, which could be rented at the beachside resort hotels. Two gentlemen are shown here riding "sailing bicycles" from the Ormond Hotel in this 1903 photograph.

The Pier and Beach Casino were constructed in 1925. The coquina footbridge across Main Street and the Pier and the Casino are all still in existence today. The Pier Casino was very popular for dancing, dining, and entertainment.

This aerial view of the beach, the pier, and the boardwalk with its coquina bandshell emphasizes how the Daytona Beach area looked in 1940. Today cars are prohibited from certain areas along the beach during the day, and there is no more night driving allowed, in an effort to protect the fragile sand dunes and wildlife.

The coquina clock tower was built in 1938, along with the Boardwalk and Bandshell, as a WPA project under Franklin Roosevelt. The tower is unique, with letters spelling out Daytona Beach in place of numbers on the clock face. A few years ago the tower was named the Sir Malcolm Campbell Clock Tower, in honor of the famous race driver.

This great shot of the Boardwalk is another Richard LeSesne photograph taken in 1940. The Bandshell at the north end of the Boardwalk was the largest open-air theater in the country at the time it was built. It drew crowds for regular band contests, talent shows, and beauty pageants, and is still used for concerts most weekends during the summer.

This image was taken as a promotion for the beach in the 1930s. By this time bathing suits had shrunk considerably, and local promoters used every opportunity to photograph young ladies for brochures to attract tourists.

This promotional beach photograph of the 1930s by LeSesne gives us an idea of the fashions of the time, as well as a look at the wonderful touring car. This image was used as an ad for clothing in a local newspaper.

Pepp's Pool was owned and operated by Harry Pepper during the 1920s. It was located on Ocean Avenue overlooking the beach, just south of the Main Street Pier. It operated as a popular attraction for tourists and locals alike from 1925 to 1937. It was surrounded by a walled structure which contained changing rooms and showers. The pool was filled with saltwater that was pumped from a long pipe extending to the ocean.

These early surfers were photographed at the beach with their longboards in 1938. The boards were large and heavy, and made by hand in manual training class at Seabreeze High School or at home. Surfing has come a long way since then, with smaller and lighter competition boards being used by surfers of all ages and sizes.

The Daytona Beach Red Cross Volunteer Lifeguard Corps was started in 1929, and operated until 1963. Today the lifeguards are Volusia County employees trained not only as lifeguards, but cross-trained as policemen. This photograph was taken at one of the large lifeguard towers in 1931.

This 1932 picture of Volunteer Lifeguards gives us an idea of the uniform of the day, as well as a look at one of their lifesaving rowboats used for rescues in rough surf.

These suntan lotion/sunburn cream ads were produced for publication by the LeSesne Studios in the 1930s. Local druggists made their own solutions and sold them over the counter at their drugstores. Paul's Drug Store and Hankins Drug Store are represented here.

Sand sailing was popular in the 1930s and 1940s. Anything with wheels and a sail would do nicely. The sport is being tried here by several young ladies near the Pier.

An early morning exercise class was being held on the beach in front of the boardwalk for residents and visitors in this 1928 photograph.

It is a busy day at the beach in this 1930s photograph taken at the Silver Beach approach. This would be a typical weekend view of cars and people on the beach at that time.

Cars are seen leaving the beach as the tide comes in after viewing one of the world-record speed runs in the 1930s.

This young man has been digging turtle eggs on the beach. It was popular to dig the eggs during turtle-nesting season, and from the eggs make soup that was considered a delicacy. Today the turtles and their nests are protected by law, and turtle soup no longer appears on restaurant menus.

The rotting timbers of the freighter *Nathan Cobb* are shown here in this 1960 photograph, taken on the beach in Ormond. The ship was a large one and broke up in the surf after running aground in 1896. There were many shipwrecks along the shores of Florida, and several wrecks were documented on the beaches of Volusia County. Among these are the schooner *Tomarko* (shown below), the steamer *Vera Cruz*, and the steamer *Commodore*. Locals salvaged goods and timber from these vessels, and many a resident has a souvenir in his or her home today from one of these ill-fated ships.

Seven

WHEELS, WINGS, AND THINGS

Miss Rowena Dean, one of the first schoolteachers in the area, is taking some of her friends for a Sunday afternoon ride along the Halifax River in this 1878 photo. Carts drawn by oxen, mules, or horses were the most common form of transportation before the turn of the century.

These four children are taking a ride in a horse-drawn wagon in this LeSesne photograph, taken in 1935.

Mr. and Mrs. R.E. Olds and friends take a ride in Daytona in a "curved dash" Oldsmobile in this image taken in February of 1902. Mr. Olds was a longtime winter resident here. He bought the former Arroyo Gardens Hotel and converted it to a residence for retired ministers and missionaries, calling it Olds Hall. It is used as a nursing home today.

Mr. William Allen is sitting in his new motorcar in front of his home on Ridgewood Avenue. Also shown are Emma Edick and Rena Belsario and her children.

This 1897 photo shows a rare tandem three-wheeled bicycle, which was manufactured by Richard Baker here in Daytona. The ladies in the picture are Mrs. Baker and her sister.

These young ladies sporting their Gibson Girl look are on a bicycling outing in 1890. They had stopped to rest under the shade of the trees near the river.

This Curtiss Pusher Aeroplane was flown by J.D. McCurdy at the Daytona Air Exhibition of March 1911 on the beach in front of the Clarendon Hotel. These activities were held for the entertainment of the winter visitors staying at the hotels.

Miss Ruth Law was the first female to pilot a plane in Florida. She flew exhibitions and took passengers on flights along the beach between 1913 and 1916. She is shown in a Curtiss Model E Pusher in this 1915 photograph.

Bill Lindley ran a passenger plane service and flying school off the beach in Daytona in the 1920s. He is shown here next to his Curtiss Jenny.

This Fourth of July picnic on the beach in 1920 shows a bi-plane surrounded by motorcars.

This huge Warner Cook steam engine was a forerunner of the tractors used today by farmers in the area.

The *Bulow* was the first train that came to Daytona on the St. Johns and Halifax River Railway, arriving on December 2, 1886. With the advent of railroad service to the area, commerce flourished, and locals were finally able to receive supplies from points north on a regular basis. The trains also brought tourists, enhancing the local economy.

Horse- or mule-drawn trolleys were used to transport passengers from the mainland across the river to the Ormond Hotel at the turn of the century. This image was taken in 1913.

Battery-operated trolleys came into use before 1920, and one is seen here on bustling South Beach Street, probably about 1914. The Burgoyne Esplanade (riverfront walkway) can be seen on the right.

One of the first limousines was billed as Mac Kay's Daytona to DeLand Ford Express. It was two 1920s Fords welded together, accommodating up to eight passengers and luggage. It is seen here heading south on Beach Street, with the Halifax River Yacht Club in the background.

Commodore and Mrs. Charles Burgoyne, standing, are seen here in this 1904 photograph taken on the beach. Dr. Sealey, who is seated behind the wheel, owned this Yale automobile, one of the first motorcars owned by a Daytona resident.

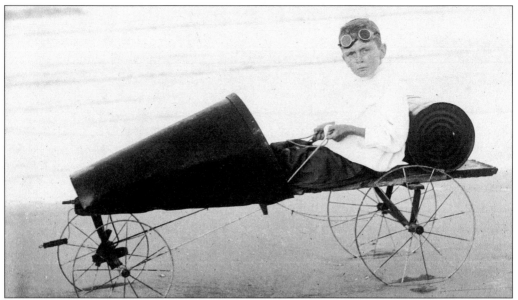

This photograph of Lawson Diggett and his push-mobile racer on the beach was taken in 1912 when he was 11 years old. This car was a forerunner of the soap box derby cars that would come along later.

Thomas Robert Ames sits in a goat cart to pose for this picture in front of the Carter Hall Hotel in Daytona Beach in 1932. These goat carts were popular props for traveling photographers, and many people took advantage of the opportunity before cameras became common place.

Eight

RIVER RAMBLINGS

A young tourist aims her rifle at an alligator while aboard the *Nemo* on a cruise on the Tomoka River in 1904. The Ormond Hotel arranged this river excursion boat tour for its guests. These boats took visitors on a trip highlighting the native wildlife and exotic plants along the river.

This ferry was the typical means to cross a river at the turn of the century until bridges were built. This ferry is crossing the Tomoka River in the early 1900s.

This steam-powered boat cruising the Tomoka River was called the *Halifax*. Its passengers this day were as follows: Charley Barnes, Hatti Higbee, Marion Blaynes, Frank Hand, Dick Wilder, Ettie Meers, Harold Tibbets, Edith Pratt, Charlotte Guard, Chris Winchell, and Captain and Mrs. D.O. Balcom.

This sleek powerboat is moored in the Halifax River just south of the South Bridge (Orange Avenue), near the Yacht Club. This picture was taken by local photographer Edward Harris in the early 1900s.

An early steam-powered sightseeing boat is seen here cruising on the Halifax River in the 1920s. The picture was taken from the dock of the Palmetto House, and the Botefuhr home can be seen on the distant shore.

Excursion boats have sailed the still waters of the Tomoka River since the late 1800s. Here the *Dixie* and the *Gleam* are docked in front of a sign that reads, "Anyone found killing alligators in this stream or on its banks will be prosecuted to the full extent of the law."

This photograph, taken in 1895, shows the *Cherokee* on the Tomoka River. It was one of the largest excursion boats, had a crew of four, and could carry about 75 passengers.

The Halifax River Yacht Club is featured prominently in the foreground of this 1920s view of the downtown Daytona area. The fire station can be seen on the south side of the bridge and the Burgoyne Casino on the north side. The Williams Hotel can be seen at the top center of the photograph.

The Halifax River Yacht Club is shown here in 1931 with a full complement of yachts moored at the docks.

The "cat boat" was standard transportation on the river for many families during the early days. They depended on these boats to pick up and deliver supplies before roads were built to the outside world.

Commodore Charles G. Burgoyne's 65-foot yacht the *Sweetheart* was one of the sleekest on the river. He had a large boathouse built adjoining his property to accommodate the yacht and had the channel dredged in the river for better access. He decked out his yacht with flags and banners on holidays and invited townsfolk for boat rides down the river.

This woman is fishing with a cane pole in the river just south of the Yacht Club. Saltwater catfish, sailor's choice, and sheepshead were usually the main catch of the day.

This photo by Harris shows the Thompson family on a boating and picnic trip on Spruce Creek in the early 1900s. Spruce Creek is still mostly undeveloped and pristine today.

The South Bridge was constructed in 1888 at what is now Orange Avenue. It was built of wood planking and had a center draw, just as it does today. When first constructed, it was a toll bridge and cost 10¢ to cross. The Gamble mansion can be seen on the right, and the cupola of Lilian's Place on the left.

Henry Flagler bought the St. Johns and Halifax River Railway and the White Railroad in 1890, and expanded them into the Florida East Coast Railroad. This bridge was the first railroad bridge crossing the Halifax River. Flagler had it built to transport visitors from the North to his great Ormond Hotel.

Major H.O.D. Segrave is seen here racing his speedboat *Miss England* in an attempt to establish a new speed record on the Halifax River in Daytona in the 1930s.

Powerboat races were popular on the Halifax River until the 1970s. This photograph shows an inboard race in progress in the 1930s.

Pleasure boating on the Halifax River has always been a popular pastime. Here a group of friends enjoys the sun and wind in their new Chris Craft boat in the early 1950s.

The 100-foot yacht, the *Carolyn*, is cruising in the ocean beyond Ponce de Leon Inlet. The Daytona Beach Boat Works and Marina serviced and docked many of these large yachts on the Halifax River over the years.

Nine
DAYTONA AT WAR

A photograph taken in Daytona during World War I shows Lt. W.F. Jibb and Lt. Fred Caldwell standing in front of the old City Hall after an exhibition drill. The building had been the train station for a time and was located at the corner of Orange Avenue and South Beach Street.

From 1942 to 1944, companies of the Women's Army Corps marched on the Boardwalk at the beach. The Saturday morning reviews proved to be popular with the locals as well as soldiers and sailors from nearby bases.

This 1942 photo shows the WAC's tent city at Bethune Point, off South Beach Street. The area was used as temporary quarters for 6,000 women at the beginning of World War II until a more permanent cantonment was built.

The WAC color guard is shown marching at the 2nd WAC Training Center at Daytona Beach.

Daytona Beach was selected as the 2nd WAC Training Center because of the year-round mild climate. The cantonment was located in the Highlands section of Daytona, which today is the site of the Halifax Hospital and Daytona Beach Community College. At the peak of the operation there were over 14,000 women in training here.

This 1945 photo shows a dive-bomber flying over the Daytona Beach Naval Air Station. On December 15, 1942, the airport here was converted into a WW II Naval Air Training Center where thousands of young men were trained to serve their country.

A World War II sub-chaser is shown here heading for Ponce de Leon Inlet to undergo sea trials before being placed into active service.

Planes from the Daytona Beach Naval Training Center are seen here practicing strafing runs along the coast during WW II. Citizens were required to black out their home windows at night due to enemy submarine activity along the Florida coast.

This is one of many launching ceremonies that took place here for U.S. Navy sub-chasers produced by the Daytona Beach Boat Works. During WW II the boat works built P.C. class 110-foot sub-chaser ships, along with 104-foot air/sea rescue vessels and 40-foot motor launches, known as Liberty Boats. The WAC Band can be seen playing in the center of the photo.

1942—

United States Citizens Defense Corps
CD   of Halifax Defense Council   CD
DAYTONA BEACH, FLORIDA

Member   **Mrs. Hoke Johnson**   EMERGENCY MEDICAL UNIT **R.N.**

Designation   **Dir of Dist 8 Unit**

Assigned Post   **EMD8FA**
       No.   Description

S. Ridgewood Sch.

Chief of ~~Department~~ unit **815 N. Grandview   932**
       Address   Phone

Director of ~~Unit~~ Dept. **211 Cedar St.   1186-J**
       Address   Phone

Commander   **502 N. Grandview   219** Phone
       Address   Phone

SPECIAL INSTRUCTIONS

1.—When the 'ALERT' sounds or Mobilization is called, go at once to your assigned post for duty.

Mrs. Hoke Johnson
                Chief of Department

George W. Pollock
                Director of Unit

There were many contributions made during the war by local non-military individuals. Many served as coastal air and sea spotters, belonged to the Civil Air Patrol, or were members of the Halifax Defense Council. Everyone contributed to the war effort by using their War Ration Coupon Books and conserving on gasoline, sugar, meat, and coffee. Victory gardens and scrap drives for paper and metal were important citizen duties too.

UNITED STATES OF AMERICA
War Ration Book One

WARNING

1 Punishments ranging as high as *Ten Years' Imprisonment or $10,000 Fine, or Both,* may be imposed under United States Statutes for violations thereof arising out of infractions of Rationing Orders and Regulations.

2 This book must not be transferred. It must be held and used only by or on behalf of the person to whom it has been issued, and anyone presenting it thereby represents to the Office of Price Administration, an agency of the United States Government, that it is being so held and so used. For any misuse of this book it may be taken from the holder by the Office of Price Administration.

3 In the event either of the departure from the United States of the person to whom this book is issued, or his or her death, the book must be surrendered in accordance with the Regulations.

4 Any person finding a lost book must deliver it promptly to the nearest Ration Board.

No. 983143 –305

OFFICE OF PRICE ADMINISTRATION

Ten

DARING MEN AND
THEIR FAST MACHINES

Race driver Barney Oldfield is giving advice to Sir Malcolm Campbell just before Campbell made his final world-record run on the beach in 1935. Campbell drove his *Bluebird V* to a record speed of 276.82 mph.

Horace T. Thomas drove the "Pirate," owned by Ransom E. Olds, and set a world record of 54.38 mph on March 26, 1903, during the first annual winter automobile racing meet. This was the beginning of racing in Ormond/Daytona.

The 200-horsepower "Durracq" car is shown here in front of the Ormond Garage. This car was driven to a world speed record of 117.64 mph by Louis Chevrolet on January 26, 1906.

Famous race driver Barney Oldfield sits in his "Blitzen Lightning Benz." He drove this car to a new world record of 131.72 mph in 1910. A grandstand at Daytona International Speedway is named for Oldfield.

Sir Malcolm Campbell poses for photographers in this 1928 shot by LeSesne. The famous monoplane *Pride of Detroit* is seen in the background. Campbell had been a captain in the British Royal Air Corps and was later knighted for his land speed accomplishments.

A crowd of spectators gathers around the control and timing tower during a land speed record run in 1932. Everyone in town would stop what they were doing to see these runs on the beach. School bells would ring, and children would be released from school!

Mechanics are pushing Major H.O.D. Segrave's "Sunbeam Mystery S" race car into position for his world-record run of 203.79 mph on March 29, 1927, making him the first man to exceed 200 mph in an automobile. He was knighted when he returned to England.

Sir Henry Segrave drove the "Golden Arrow" to 231.44 mph, establishing a world land speed record at Daytona Beach on March 11, 1929.

Young Frank Lockhart drove the "Stutz Black Hawk," which he designed and built for an attempt to set a new speed record in 1928. While driving the tiny car at a speed of over 200 mph, he was killed when his car crashed into the surf. He was only 26 years old.

Ralph Mulford sits in his car before setting a new stock car record in 1921. He drove 1 mile in 34.25 seconds.

The White "Triplex" was a huge race car powered by a trio of 12-cylinder Liberty aircraft engines, generating a combined output of 1,200 horsepower. On March 12, 1929, driver/mechanic Lee Bible was killed in a tragic crash while driving in excess of 200 mph.

This was all that was left after the crash of the "Triplex," which killed Lee Bible and newsreel cameraman Charles Traub.

Ray Keech, a local driver, drove the
"Triplex" to a new land speed
record of 207.55 mph on April 22,
1928, and brought the record back
to America.

Ralph De Palma is seen here driving the Packard race car in which he established an unofficial speed record in 1919.

The Ormond Garage was built by Henry Flagler near the Ormond Hotel in 1904 to accommodate race cars during the annual automobile meets held on the beach. The historic building was destroyed by fire on January 7, 1976.

This publicity photograph shows the pace car for the first automobile race held on the beach/road course in 1936. The driver is Doc MacKenzie.

Modified race cars cross the finish line on the back stretch for the first race held on the beach/road course in 1936.

Spectators line the beach to watch a race in progress in this photograph showing cars entering the famous north turn of the course.

This aerial view of the second beach/road course was taken from the south turn. This course opened in 1948 near Ponce de Leon Inlet and was 4.1 miles long. This course replaced the first beach/road course, which was built in 1936, was 3.2 miles long, and was located farther north on the beach.

Hometown boy Glenn "Fireball" Roberts became Daytona Beach's most popular race car driver. He always gave the thrill-seeking audience what they came to see. Roberts rose to fame driving the black and gold #22 Pontiac owned by Ray Stevens and prepared by local mechanic Smokey Yunick. The 35-year-old driver was killed in a crash in 1964 at Charlotte Motor Speedway.

Fireball Roberts is seen here early in his career, after winning a race with his modified sportster sponsored by the local Fish Carburetor Corp.

Race cars are rounding the north turn in this 1936 race on the beach/road course. The course was hazardous for the drivers because of the deep ruts continuously carved into the sand during the race.

Spectators fill the grand stand at the north turn of an early beach/road course race. Many other fans avoided paying the admission by climbing over the palmetto-covered and rattlesnake-infested sand dunes!

Speedy Thompson is at the wheel of his race car that he named "the Little Jewel." Thompson was a fierce competitor at the early races and a favorite of fans.

Local filling station owner Bill France stands in front of his race car before the start of the 1936 race. France finished the race in fifth place. He went on to become a race promoter, founder of NASCAR, and the builder of the Daytona Beach International Speedway. No other individual has contributed more to the sport of automobile racing.

Herb Thomas is rounding the south turn on the beach course driving his modified stock car. Thomas went on to win 49 NASCAR Winston Cup races and was the first driver to win two season championships in 1951 and 1953.

Cars are lining up for the start of the 1950 Winston Cup race on the beach. Tim Flock's #90 Cadillac is at the far left. Flock went on to win two Winston Cup Series Championships while driving Chryslers.

Local boy Marshall Teague graduated from Seabreeze High School in 1939. After serving in WW II, he returned to operate a Pure Oil service station and became engrossed in auto racing. He obtained sponsorship from the Hudson Motor Car Company and went on to win many stock car races during the 1950s driving his "Fabulous Hudson Hornet." Teague was killed in a crash in 1959 at the age of 37 at the new Daytona Speedway.

Marshall Teague, winner of seven NASCAR Winston Cup races, is seen driving his "Fabulous Hudson Hornet" on the beach/road course.

A motorcyclist takes a spill at the north turn of the beach/road course. Motorcycle racing became popular about the same time as auto racing in Daytona.

John Tafin sits astride his Indian motorcycle before a race on the beach in the early 1950s.

This 1956 photograph shows cars rounding the north turn of the beach/road course. Tim Flock won the race, driving a Chrysler.

Fonty Flock is shown posing with his Kiekhaefer-sponsored Dodge during a 1956 Speed Weeks promotion.

This image shows the start of the Daytona 500 race in the mid-1960s. David Pearson, who was called the Silver Fox, is driving his #21 Ford at the far left. Pearson's career included 105 NASCAR Winston Cup wins and 3 season titles.

This aerial view shows the Daytona Beach International Speedway as it appeared when it first opened in 1959. The Daytona Beach Regional Airport is seen behind the race track, and the Daytona Beach Kennel Club can be seen at the bottom right, on what is now International Speedway Boulevard.

Acknowledgments

We would like to thank those individuals who helped put this book together. Elizabeth Wills was our anchor, organizer, and advisor—we couldn't have managed without her. Donald Gaby and Elysha Dunagan aided us with research. Thanks to PS Printing for copying photographs for us. We would also like to offer special thanks to Elizabeth Sarver and Mary McFall for the loan of some photographs.

Most of all, we wish to thank the Halifax Historical Society for the wonderful photographs used in this book. The majority of the photos came from the Museum's vast collection, which has been donated by the generous descendants of the area's pioneer families. Local professional photographers from years gone by took the majority of the photographs used in this book. Those photographers are Edward G. Harris, Richard LeSesne, and William Coursen. This book is complemented by their wonderful images.

Bibliography

Booth, Fred. *Early Days in Daytona Beach, Florida, How a City Was Founded.* 1951.

Clarida, Vince. *Charles Grover Burgoyne, The Man Who Brought Tourism to Daytona.* 1997.

Fitzgerald, T.E. *Volusia County Past and Present.* 1937.

Punnett, Dick. *Racing on the Rim.* 1997.

Punnett, Dick and Yvonne. *Thrills, Chills, and Spills.* 1990.

Strickland, Alice. *Ormond on the Halifax, A Centennial History of Ormond Beach, Florida.* 1995.

Tiller, Jim and Tom Tucker. *Daytona, The Quest for Speed.* 1994.

Vertical files at the Halifax Historical Museum.